IMAGES OF WAR

THE BATTLE FOR THE CRIMEA 1941–1944

Considered a military backwater, the bulk of the Red Army's tanks in the Crimea consisted of old T-26, such as the one seen here, and BT-5 tanks. Both had come into service in the early 1930s.

IMAGES OF WAR

THE BATTLE FOR THE CRIMEA 1941–1944

RARE PHOTOGRAPHS FROM WARTIME ARCHIVES

Anthony Tucker-Jones

Pen & Sword
MILITARY

First published in Great Britain in 2016 by
PEN & SWORD MILITARY
an imprint of
Pen & Sword Books Ltd,
47 Church Street,
Barnsley,
South Yorkshire
S70 2AS

A CIP record for this book is available from the British Library.

ISBN 978 1 47386 730 8

Typeset by CHIC GRAPHICS

Printed and bound by CPI Group (UK) Ltd, Croydon, CR0 4YY

Pen & Sword Books Ltd incorporates the imprints of Pen & Sword Archaeology,
Atlas, Aviation, Battleground, Discovery, Family History, History, Maritime, Military,
Naval, Politics, Railways, Select, Social History, Transport, True Crime, Claymore
Press, Frontline Books, Leo Cooper, Praetorian Press, Remember When, Seaforth
Publishing and Wharncliffe.

For a complete list of Pen & Sword titles please contact
Pen & Sword Books Limited
47 Church Street, Barnsley, South Yorkshire, S70 2AS, England
E-mail: enquiries@pen-and-sword.co.uk
Website: www.pen-and-sword.co.uk

Contents

Introduction

When Adolf Hitler invaded the Soviet Union his armies charged into Byelorussia through the cities of Minsk and Smolensk toward Moscow. In the north they swept through the tiny Baltic States to the very gates of Leningrad. In Ukraine Hitler's forces stormed into Kiev and Kharkov. In the very far south German troops and their Romanian allies fought their way to the Black Sea port of Odessa and thrust into the Crimea.

Of all the battles fought on the Eastern Front, the battle for the Crimea was one of the most desperate. Thanks to the Crimea's geography it was very difficult for both sides to feed in reinforcements and supplies to the battlefield. In a series of operations the Germans subdued Soviet resistance despite the Red Army's heroic efforts to hold the naval base of Sevastopol. It took the Axis forces ten long months to conquer the Crimea in 1941-42. In particular the Soviet defenders of Sevastopol held out for 250 days.

The German high command considered the campaigns in the Crimea as a sideshow, much as they did with North Africa. They felt it to be largely irrelevant in the greater scheme of things. Operation *Orkan* (Hurricane) was designed to take the great fortress of Sevastopol from the Red Army. This was the responsibility of Field Marshal Fedor von Bock's Army Group South as a preliminary to Operation *Blau* which was to be launched along the length of the Eastern Front in the summer of 1942.

Clearing the Soviets from the Crimea was a necessity to protect Army Group South's right flank. It would also facilitate the German 11th Army crossing from the Crimea into the Taman Peninsula to support 1st Panzer Army and 17th Army in their offensive along the eastern coast of the Black Sea after sweeping across the lower reaches of the Rivers Don and Donets.

Field Marshal Erich von Manstein, who commanded the German forces in Crimea, was fulsome in his praise of their fighting abilities:

In attack and pursuit their aggressive spirit was unparalleled; and when the situation appeared hopeless they would stand and fight unflinchingly. Often they may have not known what compelled us to make demands on them that seemed impossible to fulfil, or why they were flung from one action to another and from one front to the next. And yet they went to the very limit of endurance to carry out these demands, reciprocating the trust of those who led them.

What made the fighting in Crimea so remarkable was that it was one of the few instances where a German army fought a battle without any real interference from Hitler. Thanks to its isolated geography the Axis forces committed to the battle for the Crimea in 1941 were able to operate independently. As Manstein recalled:

> It was a campaign which, in ten months of incessant fighting, included both offensive and defensive battles, mobile warfare with full freedom of action, a headlong pursuit operation, landings by an enemy in control of the sea, partisan engagements and an assault on a powerfully defended fortress.

The Crimean land mass is almost an island, attached to the mainland by two narrow land bridges to the north and one to the east. As the war progressed, Axis forces stationed in Russia and Ukraine going home on leave or being medically evacuated had to travel huge distances by road or rail. In Crimea the easiest way out was across the Black Sea to Odessa in the Ukraine or Constanta in Romania, but that meant running the gauntlet of the Soviet Navy.

When the Red Army launched a series of counteroffensives in late 1943, Axis forces were cut off in the Crimea. Hitler stuck to his normal ridiculous dictat that no ground must be relinquished and that the garrison should stay put until relieved. In 1944 the Red Army liberated the Crimea and Sevastopol in the space of just four days. The German and Romanian units were left to face a terrible fate, culminating in an Axis version of Dunkirk with an evacuation fleet sailing for the Romanian port of Constanta. The Soviet air forces and navy contested their passage with bloody results. Only the bravery of the Romanian Royal Navy ensured that tens of thousands of Axis troops were rescued from the Khersones Peninsula.

For those German, Romanian and Soviet soldiers who survived the terrible battles fought in the Crimea, the killing grounds of the Perekop Isthmus, Sivash Sea and the Kerch Straits were forever burned into their memories.

Photograph Sources

All the images in this book are courtesy of the Scott Pick WWII Russian Front Original Photo Collection. This consists of almost 2,500 black and white photographs. They provide a remarkable and often grim insight into the many aspects of the war on the Eastern Front. Notably, the quality of the photographs is consistently high throughout the archive. Most of those selected by the author to illustrate this title have never been published before. Pen & Sword and the author are indebted to Scott Pick for his generous assistance with this project.

Chapter One

The Road to Sevastopol

In the wake of Hitler's invasion of the Soviet Union the Romanian 4th Army moved over the Dniester River on 3 August 1941, with the intention of occupying the Ukrainian Black Sea port of Odessa. The Romanians were given this task on the assumption that the Soviet garrison, known as the Separate Coastal Army, would quickly surrender once hemmed in. Things did not go according to plan and the fierce Soviet resistance did not bode well for the capture of Sevastopol in the Crimea.

Although the Romanian Air Force fought well against the Red Army and Red Air Force, crucially it was unable to prevent the Soviet Black Sea Fleet from supporting Odessa. In addition the small Romanian Navy was outnumbered and outclassed by the much bigger Soviet fleet. This meant that it was held back to protect the shipping routes in and out of the Romanian port of Constanta and through the Bosporus into the Mediterranean. Nonetheless, two Romanian torpedo boats managed to intercept a Soviet destroyer south of Odessa on the night of 18 August 1941 and damaged it.

Such successes were limited. By the end of the month the Romanians had suffered almost 30,000 casualties and were held outside Odessa by the Soviet main line of defence. The Romanian assault was resumed on 12 September with the assistance of pioneer and artillery units from the German 11th Army. Two days later the attack was hampered by a shortage of artillery ammunition. The Black Sea Fleet continued to bring in reinforcements and supplies and the Separate Coastal Army held out for another month before being evacuated to Sevastopol.

The destruction of the Red Army across the western Soviet Union in the summer of 1941 was not good for the morale of the Soviet garrison in the Crimea. Nonetheless, the German conquest of the region was certainly not a forgone conclusion. Crucially, unlike the Crimean war of 1854-56 when the Western Powers had naval supremacy, in 1941 the Soviet navy and air force dominated the Black Sea and the Sea of Azov.

The combined Axis forces had to fight a campaign on two fronts, first with the breakthrough at Perekop into northern Crimea and the Battle on the Sea of Azov. From 26 September 1941 the Axis forces launched an operation that successfully occupied most of the Crimea with the exception of Sevastopol, which like Odessa continued to hold out against the Axis armies.

General Erich von Manstein arrived to take command at the headquarters of 11th Army in Nikolayev, the Soviet naval base at the mouth of the Bug on 17 September 1941. He replaced Colonel General Eugen Ritter von Schobert who had been killed after his reconnaissance aircraft crashed in a Soviet minefield. Manstein was pleased by what he found, noting that 11th Army's operations staff 'was almost without exception a superb team'.

He also found he had responsibility for the Romanian 3rd Army. In theory the Axis forces committed to the invasion of the Soviet Union from Romania, comprising the German 11th and Romanian 3rd and 4th Armies, were under the direction of the Romanian leader Marshal Antonescu, who answered to Army Group South under Field Marshal von Rundstedt. By the time Manstein arrived only the Romanian 4th Army remained under Antonescu, while the 3rd Army under the command of General Dumitrescu had been subordinated to the German 11th Army.

Manstein was not impressed by the Romanian military; the bulk of their troops were drawn from the peasantry, which meant that their overall level of education was poor. Crucially, they lacked adequate combat training. Manstein felt that most of the officers were not up to the job and there was an absence of recognisable non-commissioned officers. Worryingly their weapons were largely obsolete, especially their anti-tank guns, leaving them vulnerable to Soviet tank attack. The Romanian Army, having regained Bessarabia, had no stomach for marching further into the Soviet Union.

Upon Manstein's arrival the staff at 11th Army HQ briefed him on the current situation. The army constituted the southernmost wing of the sprawling Eastern Front. Their area of operations ran from the Dnieper bend south of Zaporozhye down into the Crimea. Manstein found that after the forests of northern Russia his region of responsibility was ideal for tank warfare – except that 11th Army had no panzers.

Manstein's task was twofold; he had to keep the pressure on the Red Army as it retreated eastwards. This required the bulk of his troops, consisting of General Salmuth's 30th Corps and General Kübler's 49th Mountain Corps, to push along the northern coast of the Sea of Azov toward Rostov. At the same time he was expected to subdue Soviet resistance in the Crimea, employing General Hansen's 54th Corps. This was vital to prevent the Red Air Force using its Crimean air bases from which they could attack Romania's vital oilfields. Once Crimea was secured those forces detached from 11th Army were expected to cross the Straits of Kerch to support the offensive beyond Rostov.

Despite a major concentration of Red Air Force units in the region, Soviet air attacks were little more than a nuisance. The Soviet intention was to draw enemy aircraft away from the Ukrainian capital of Kiev and Uman. To this end by 9 July 1941 they had conducted over 5,000 sorties in the Romanian border area. Luftwaffe units in Romania shot down 143 aircraft between 22 June 1941 and 21 October, half of which had been caught by anti-aircraft guns. When six Soviet bombers did reach the Romanian oil refineries on 13 July only two returned home, showing that there was no urgent need to redeploy German or Romanian fighter units from the front line.

The German 22nd Infantry Division had forced a crossing of the Dnieper at Berislavl in early September 1941, which meant splitting 11th Army's resources by pushing both southward and eastward. The Sivash, or 'Lazy Sea', separated the Crimea from the mainland; this was largely too deep for infantry to cross but too shallow for assault boats. The only land approaches from the north were by the Perekop Isthmus to the west and a strip of land running west of Genichesk to the east of the sea. The latter was a narrow causeway linked by numerous bridges and wholly unsuitable for an attack. The Perekop was less than five miles wide and well defended by field works ten miles deep and the ancient Tartars' Ditch (also known as the Turkish Ditch). Even if the Perekop could be overcome, at Ishun salt lakes reduced the front to a width of just two miles.

Manstein immediately appreciated that the two divisions belonging to 54th Corps would not be sufficient to defeat the Soviet garrison defending the Perekop. He decided to make capturing the Crimea a priority and reinforced 54th Corps with the German Mountain Corps which would be ideal for fighting in the mountainous southern Crimea. His preparations were not completed until 24 September but two days later his troops had taken the Perekop and crossed the Tartars' Ditch. The Red Army was driven back between the Ishun Lakes with the Germans capturing 10,000 prisoners, 112 tanks and 135 guns.

In the meantime to the northeast of the Crimea the Red Army counter-attacked between the Dnieper and Melitopol. This sparked the Battle for the Sea of Azov. While Manstein 30th Corps held, the Soviets overran the Romanian 4th Mountain Brigade and opened a ten-mile-wide gap in the Romanian 3rd Army's front. Manstein had no option but to redeploy the German Mountain Corps to assist the Romanians. In early October 30th Corps and the Romanian Army in cooperation with the 1st Panzer Group driving from the north struck back. They successfully trapped the Soviets at Bol Tokmak, capturing 65,000 prisoners, 125 tanks and 500 guns.

Following this victory, 1st Panzer Group was tasked with pushing on Rostov and 11th Army instructed to concentrate on conquering the Crimea, using the 30th and 54th Corps. They were reinforced by the 42nd Corps which consisted of two infantry divisions. The Romanian Army reverted to the control of Marshal Antonescu and deployed for coastal defence on the Black Sea and Sea of Azov. However, Manstein persuaded Antonescu to let him take the Romanian Mountain Corps into the Crimea.

The Soviets also reinforced the Crimea. On 16 October 1941 they evacuated Odessa, which had been holding off the Romanian 4th Army, and transferred the garrison to Sevastopol by sea. The Luftwaffe did all it could to prevent this but Manstein now found his six divisions facing ten Soviet ones. In the Crimea the Soviets also had large numbers of tanks whereas 11th Army had none.

Manstein could only initially commit the 73rd, 46th and 22nd Infantry Divisions under the command of 54th Corps to forcing the Soviet defences at Ishun. The salt flats of Ishun offered no cover and the skies were dominated by the Red Air Force. Soviet air attacks got so bad that German anti-aircraft batteries stopped firing for fear of the consequences. For ten days Manstein's infantry fought to the point of exhaustion but on 28 October the Soviet defences gave way.

Under the codename Operation *Trappenfang* (Bustard Trap) the 11th Army poured south in hot pursuit and by 16 November 1941 controlled all of the Crimea except for Sevastopol. Two Soviet armies, comprising twelve rifle and four cavalry divisions, had been smashed. The Red Army had deployed 200,000 men in the Crimea, over half of whom had been captured along with 160 tanks and 700 guns. The survivors either fled into Sevastopol or across the Straits of Kerch to the mainland.

(Opposite, above) General Erich von Manstein, centre, photographed in June 1941. Two months later he was assigned command of the German 11th Army with the task of securing the Crimea and the Sea of Azov.

(Opposite, below) German troops examining a knocked out Soviet T-26 light tank, which were used extensively in the Crimea. The German Army Group South cut through the Red Army forces in the Ukraine very swiftly in the summer of 1941.

German infantry advancing through Russian cornfields. Fighting at Melitopol diverted from Manstein's main effort against the Crimea.

(*Opposite, above*) German infantry crossing a pontoon bridge spanning the Dnieper. Once the German 11th Army was over the river it made the position of the Soviet garrison in the Crimea precarious.

(*Opposite, below*) Manstein captured 10,000 Soviet prisoners during his attack on the Perekop in northern Crimea in September 1941. Most of these men are wearing the 1935 khaki cloth side cap called the *pilotka*.

Yet more Soviet prisoners. Following the Red Army's counter-attack between the Dnieper and Melitopol German and Romanian troops captured 65,000 Soviet troops at Bol Tokmak.

German sightseers examine a Soviet KV-1 heavy tank – its turret is laying upside-down to the right

Two more knocked-out KV tanks. Whilst a sound design in theory, in practice it proved no match for the panzers.

The Soviet KV-2, armed with a 152mm gun, proved to be more of a liability than an asset.

Cheerful-looking German officers: securing the northern coast of the Sea of Azov left Manstein free to resume his attack on the Crimea unhindered.

A job well done – a German corporal is decorated by his young platoon commander.

In the meantime the Romanian 4th Army was advancing on Odessa to the west of the Crimea. In early August 1941 Romanian troops took some of their first Soviet PoWs at Katargy.

German infantry take a break in the summer of 1941.

More German troops taking a break. The German 11th Army had to redeploy some units to assist the Romanians held up outside Odessa.

A Soviet howitzer defending Odessa – the garrison consisted of the Separate Coastal Army. The gunners are wearing the Model 1940 helmet.

A Soviet Ch TZ-S-65 Stalinets artillery tractor on the streets of Odessa. These were produced in Chelyabinsk east of the Urals.

Somewhat bemused-looking Soviet civilians. The Soviet Separate Coastal Army left Odessa for Sevastopol in mid-October 1941, leaving most of the population to their fate.

Romanian infantry marching into Odessa unopposed.

These Soviet soldiers are inspecting the wreckage of a Romanian-built IAR-80 fighter, which went into service with the Royal Romanian Air Force in early 1941. This type of aircraft flew in support of the Romanian 3rd and 4th Armies.

A German convoy snakes its way past an abandoned Soviet BT-7 fast tank. Once Axis forces were east of the Dneiper River the fate of the Crimea was sealed.

Chapter Two

Sevastopol Besieged

In the meantime the first large-scale maritime tragedy of the Crimean campaign occurred. Despite the superiority of the Soviet Black Sea Fleet for a time the Luftwaffe ruled the skies. The Soviet hospital ship *Armenia* arrived at Sevastopol in early November 1941 with the task of evacuating wounded and non-essential personnel. After taking on board thousands of people on the night of 6/7 November the vessel was directed to Yalta, a port just to the east of Sevastopol. Once it had taken on more passengers the *Armenia* left Yalta escorted by two fighters and two armed boats.

Some 25 miles out the Luftwaffe attacked the *Armenia* despite the vessel bearing the symbol of the International Red Cross. A single He 111 bomber dropped two torpedoes: one missed but the other broke the *Armenia* in half. The ship sank within four minutes taking up to 7,000 people with it – there were just eight survivors. Three days later Stuka dive-bombers caught the cruiser *Chervona Ukraina* in the South Bay of Sevastopol. She did not sink until 13 November, giving the crew plenty of time to abandon ship.

Following the initial seizure of the Crimea, at the end of November 1941 Manstein turned his attentions to taking the Red Army's last remaining stronghold at Sevastopol. The Russian winter came to the defenders' rescue, forcing a three-week delay in the German assault. On the mainland the frost cut supplies to the Axis forces in the Crimea. Four of the five trains available south of the Dnieper were immobilised by the weather. This meant that 11th Army only got one or two trainloads of supplies a day. Furthermore, in the Crimea heavy rain made the roads impassable. Manstein had planned to open his attack on 27 November, but this slipped to 17 December.

Manstein's 54th and 30th Corps attacked Sevastopol's northern and southern defences respectively. Unfortunately the former had lost its reserve division due to the fighting around Rostov. Manstein had to force the Soviets from their forward defences between Kacha and Belbek as well as capturing their strongpoints in the Belbek valley. Then the Germans could push south of Belbek to Severnaya Bay.

Under Lieutenant General Wolff the 22nd Infantry Division fought their way in between Kacha and Belbek then stormed the heights south of the Belbek Valley along with the 132nd Infantry Division. In contrast the 50th and 24th Infantry Divisions, pushing toward Severnaya Bay, found it difficult to make progress in the mountains. By the end of December German troops had reached Fort Stalin. Colonel von Choltiz's 16th Infantry Regiment serving with the 22nd Infantry Division got into the fort's outer defences but did not capture it.

At that very moment the Red Army struck across the Straits of Kerch, threatening the German position in eastern Crimea. Once it became clear that this was no diversionary operation, Manstein had no option but to withdraw his troops on the northern front to the heights north of the Balbek Valley. Hitler was not happy about this withdrawal or that the first attempt to take Sevastopol had failed.

Only after defeating the Red Army in the Kerch Peninsula in the spring of 1942, was Manstein in a position to resume his attempts at capturing Sevastopol. He knew that if he did not do this half of the 11th Army would continue to be bogged down in the Crimea. To protect his rear Manstein detailed 42nd Corps to guard Kerch and the south coast of the Crimea. This consisted solely of the German 46th Infantry Division supported by the Romanian 7th Corps (consisting of two infantry divisions, a mountain division and a cavalry brigade). All other units were directed toward the assault on Sevastopol.

The port city was a tough nut to crack. Commanded by Lieutenant General Ivan Petrov the garrison of Sevastopol was formed by the Separate Coastal Army, consisting of 106,000 men organised into seven infantry divisions and a single dismounted cavalry division supported by three marine infantry brigades under Vice Admiral F. S. Oktabrsky. Two additional infantry brigades were landed during the battle, giving the Soviets an overall strength of about seventy battalions. In reality some 20 per cent of Petrov's command was made up of sailors from the Black Sea Fleet, most of whom were not trained to fight as infantry. Petrov's best units were considered to be the 95th, 109th, 172nd and 388th Rifle Divisions as these were the strongest. Each of them numbered about 7,000 men while the other divisions had about 5,000 men. The maritime brigades were also reasonably trained and equipped. Although the Red Air Force and Soviet Naval Aviation deployed over half a dozen fighter regiments, in fact they had very few aircraft.

The Black Sea Fleet did all it could to keep Sevastopol supplied from the Caucasian ports. However, Axis planes, torpedo boats, submarines and long-range siege guns blockaded the sea routes into the city. These caused heavy losses to the vessels of the Black Sea Fleet which included cruisers and destroyers assigned to defend the port. What supplies came in had to be carried at great risk aboard warships and submarines. Nonetheless, in June alone over 24,000 reinforcements and 15,000 tons of freight was delivered and 25,000 sick and wounded were evacuated from the beleaguered city.

Sevastopol's defences, which were divided into four sectors, were formidable comprising some 3,600 fortifications, both permanent and temporary, covering a depth of some fifteen miles around the city. These were strengthened with 600 guns and mortars, including four 305mm guns in two twin turrets. Unfortunately for the defenders ammunition was low and shells had to be used sparingly. In addition they only had thirty-eight tanks, most of them obsolete, and just fifty-three aircraft.

The Red Army had been granted a six-month breathing space in which to strengthen their defences. The local geography aided the defenders as much as their fortifications which ran from the Belbek Valley to the Black Sea coast. While the northern defences ran south from Belbek, to the north there were strongpoints particularly around Lyubimovka. The valley was covered by a battery of massive 305mm guns housed in an armoured emplacement dubbed by the Germans 'Maxim Gorky I'. The slopes were protected by a mile-deep network of fieldworks – some of which were cast from concrete.

South of Lyubimovka and Belbek were a series of strongpoints christened 'Stalin', 'Volga', 'Siberia', 'Molotov', 'GPU' and 'Cheka' by the Germans, which were linked by trenches and emplacements. The final barrier to the northern shore of Severnaya Bay was presented by another chain of strongpoints that included 'Donetz', 'Don' and 'Lenin', as well as the defences at Bartenyevka, the old North Fort and the Battery Headland coastal batteries.

A mile and a quarter east of the village of Belbek was the junction of the eastern defences with the hinge southwards protected by the Kamyshly Ravine. The slopes of the Vaila Mountains were covered in dense undergrowth these ended in steep cliffs south of Gaytany. The southern defences were protected by a series of summits that had been converted into strongpoints. Behind them were the fortified village of Kamary and the rocky massif north-east of the Bay of Balaclava. North of the road from Sevastopol is the massif of the Feyukiny Heights which extend to the coastal rage. To the west of Balaclava was the 'Maxim Gorky II' battery. There was also a wide semi-circle of defences around the city itself. Manstein knew even if they broke through the Soviets' outer defences the Red Army would still hold out in the city and on the Khersones headland.

The Soviet cruiser *Komintern* and submarine *Shch-209*. The Axis' ability to control the Black Sea was greatly hampered by the Soviet Black Sea Fleet, which included an elderly battleship, cruisers, destroyers, motor torpedo boats and submarines.

The *Komintern*, reclassified a minelayer in 1941, provided support with her 120mm guns during the sieges of Odessa and Sevastopol and the Red Army's Kerch-Feodosiya operation.

The *Fidonisy* class destroyer *Nyezamozhnik*, bristling with 102mm guns, also served with the Black Sea Fleet. Aside from patchy air cover, Soviet naval forces lacked amphibious warfare capabilities, which meant warships and requisitioned passenger ferries had to be used for hazardous landing operations.

Another view of the *Nyezamozhnik*. In 1941 the Black Sea Fleet operated from Odessa, Sevastopol, Novorossiyk, Poti and Batumi.

Photographed in the summer of 1941 this German infantryman looks tired and not altogether happy at having his picture taken. He is wearing the standard field service uniform of the German Army. The task of capturing the Crimea fell to 11th Army's infantry divisions, as they had no supporting panzers.

Soviet troops defending a hilltop trench line. Once Manstein had forced the Soviet defences on the Perekop isthmus in late October 1941 the road to Sevastopol was opened.

On 7 November 1941 a German bomber sank the Soviet hospital ship *Armenia* after she had taken on passengers from Sevastopol and Yalta. Up to 7,000 people perished, making it one of the worst maritime disasters in history.

German dive-bombers caught the Soviet cruiser *Chervona Ukraina* at Sevastopol on 12 November 1941. She sank the following day, giving the crew time to abandon ship.

The Black Sea Fleet cruiser *Krasnyi Krym* assisted with the evacuation of Odessa and provided covering fire for Soviet troops withdrawing into Sevastopol. She was also involved in the Kerch-Feodosiya operation and ferried reinforcements to Sevastopol.

Soviet prisoners help move a wounded comrade. According to Manstein, by 16 November 1941 11th Army had captured over 100,000 Soviet prisoners along with 160 tanks and 700 guns.

Red Army prisoners gathered under a statue of Lenin. 11th Army moved its headquarters to Simferopol, the capital of the Crimea on the northern edge of the Yaila Mountains. Manstein's tactical HQ was set up at Zarabus just to the north of the city.

Another tribute to Lenin. Manstein described Simferopol as a 'largely Russianised' city.

A German medic tends Soviet wounded while local womenfolk look on.

German infantry struggle to move up for an attack. During the winter in the Crimea rain rather than snow tended to obstruct operations. Bad weather meant that Manstein had to delay his attack on Sevastopol from 27 November to 17 December 1941.

A German field kitchen struggles through the mud.

Tough-looking German troops clearly prepared for the weather. Manstein's aim at the end of 1941 was to gain control of Severnaya Bay to the north of Sevastopol. Despite some gains in the Sevastopol area, Manstein was obliged to break off his attack following the Soviet landings at Kerch and Feodisiya.

A German semi-track or half-track gives a lorry a tow. Bad weather greatly hampered the redeployment of the 11th Army eastward to Kerch.

A German machine-gun team keep watch for the Red Army. In the Crimean mountains bands of partisans and Red Army stragglers proved to be a problem for the occupying forces.

Soviet PoWs are escorted to the rear. After the capture of the Crimea, Soviet troops either withdrew into Sevastopol, escaped across the Kerch straits or fled into the Crimean mountains.

The best way to travel during the Russian winter. The cold weather on the mainland cut German supplies to their troops in the Crimea.

Chapter Three

Battle of the Kerch Peninsula

The Red Army spent over a month preparing to counter-attack in the Crimea. Their plan was to relieve Sevastopol by striking from the east. On 26 December 1941 the Soviets landed 13,000 men on the Kerch peninsula in eastern Crimea and on 29 December conducted another landing with 3,000 men near the port of Feodosiya to the southwest supported by the Black Sea Fleet.

The units involved were Lieutenant General V. N. Lvov's 51st Army and Lieutenant General S. I. Chenyak's 44th Army; they were part of General D. T. Kozlov's Transcaucasus Front (later the Caucasus Front and from 28 January 1942, after its move into the Kerch area, the Crimean Front). They had chosen the exact moment that 11th Army was making its first assault on the defences of Sevastopol. Manstein had committed all his forces except for one German division and two Romanian brigades and was faced with an unwelcome dilemma.

At Sevastopol Manstein wanted to gain command of Severnaya Bay, so initially only 30th Corps was ordered to break off the attack. The German 170th Infantry Division was sent to the threatened Kerch peninsula. Meanwhile 5th Corps pressed on with its northern attack on Sevastopol with the aim of reaching Severnaya Bay. By 30 December it was clear that this could not be achieved and the assault was called off.

Manstein knew he had no choice as Soviet radio intercepts showed that the Kerch attack was an all-out offensive to recapture the Crimea and destroy 11th Army. Once over the Straits of Kerch the Red Army began landing two divisions either side of the city of Kerch. Defending the peninsula was Lieutenant General Hans Graf von Sponeck's 42nd Corps, which consisted only of the 46th Infantry Division. Sponeck wanted to evacuate the peninsula with the aim of sealing it off at its narrowest point at Parpach to the northeast of Feodosiya.

Manstein refused, as he did not want the Red Army getting a bridgehead at Kerch that could create a second front in the Crimea. Instead of retreating, Sponeck was ordered to attack. At the same time the 4th and 8th Romanian Mountain Brigades along with the German 213th Infantry Regiment were deployed to Feodosiya. By 28 December Sponeck's troops had eliminated the Soviet footholds north and south of Kerch – except for an enclave on the northern shore.

That night the Red Army landed at Feodosiya just before the Romanians arrived. This put Soviet troops in a position from which they could drive along the Crimea's southern coast westward through Yalta and on to Sevastopol. Sponeck, alarmed by this new landing to his rear, ordered an immediate evacuation of Kerch. Meanwhile the Romanian Mountain Corps failed to stop the Soviets at Feodosiya and Soviet tanks pushed it back east of Stary Krim. From 29 December the Soviets landed another 23,000 men at Feodosiya.

Sponeck's 46th Infantry Division, abandoning much of its equipment on the icy roads, reached Parpach. Along with the 23rd Infantry Regiment and available Romanian troops they established defensive positions between the northern slopes of the Yalia Mountains near Stary Krim and the Sivash west of Ak-Monai.

By 15 January 1942 Manstein was ready to counter-attack the eight Soviet divisions at Feodosiya. This was a gamble as the 30th and 42nd Corps could only muster three and a half weak German divisions and a single Romanian mountain brigade. In addition the weather had closed in over Feodosiya thereby keeping the Luftwaffe at bay. Nonetheless the Germans pressed home their attack and by 18 January the Soviet bridgehead had been crushed. The Red Army suffered 6,700 dead and 10,000 captured along with eighty-five tanks and 177 guns. Despite the loss of this port the Soviets were still able to build up their forces at Kerch by crossing the ice from the Taman Peninsula and the Kuban.

Manstein wanted to press on and drive the Soviets from Kerch but the panzer battalion and two bombers wings he had been promised were diverted elsewhere on the mainland. Instead 11th Army worked on driving the Soviets back to the Parpach bottleneck with a view to sealing off the Kerch peninsula between the Black Sea and the Sea of Azov. Elsewhere the Red Army was counter-attacking trying to regain ground lost the previous summer. Manstein's aerial reconnaissance indicated that the Red Army and Red Air Force were building up their forces in the Black Sea harbours and in the airfields north of the Caucasus. By late January 1942 Manstein's intelligence indicated that there were nine Soviet divisions on the Parpach front supported by two rifle brigade groups and two independent tank brigades.

The Red Army opened its offensive on the Parpach front on 27 February 1942 and fighting resumed at Sevastopol. The Soviets paused on 3 March and then resumed their attack again ten days later employing eight divisions and the two tank brigades. In the first three days of bitter fighting the German 46th Infantry division beat off repeated attacks and knocked out 136 enemy tanks. Manstein finally found 11th Army had been allotted armoured support with the arrival of the newly-formed 22nd Panzer Division. This inexperienced unit was thrown into a counter-attack supported by the 46th and 170th Infantry Divisions on 20 March, but it proved a failure and the panzers were pulled out of the line for a rest and refit.

On 26 March and again on 9 April the Red Army units of the Crimean Front in the Kerch expended the last of their offensive capacity against tough resistance. In particular, the latter attack was supported by 160 tanks but was still beaten off by 42nd Corps. By late April while Sevastopol continued to be defended by the Soviet Coastal Army, Kerch was held by the 44th and 51st Armies. These included seventeen rifle divisions, two cavalry divisions and four independent armoured brigades.

For his counteroffensive, codenamed Operation *Trappenjagd* (Bustard Hunt), Manstein gathered just five German infantry divisions and 22nd Panzer. These were reinforced by the newly arrived Romanian 7th Corps (consisting of the Romanian 10th and 19th Divisions and the Romanian 8th Cavalry brigade). In early May 1942 the Luftwaffe's 8th Air Corps from Luftflotte 4 arrived in the Crimea under General Wolfram Freiherr von Richthofen. Once the Luftwaffe's fighters had driven away the Red Air Force it was able to establish air superiority over Parpach and Kerch then set about the Red Army with its bombers. The Soviet Crimean Front now fielded Major General K. S. Kolganov's 47th Army as well as the 44th and 51st Armies.

Intelligence showed that the Red Army had massed two-thirds of its forces in the northern sector which curved west to Kiet. Rather than tackle this, Manstein proposed to attack along the southern coast using 30th Corps consisting of the 28th Light, 50th and 132nd Infantry Divisions and the tanks of the 22nd Panzer Division. The 170th Infantry Division although holding the central part of the front was assigned a follow through role on the southern front. The attack was supported by the Luftwaffe which strangled the Red Army's supply lines into Kerch.

It was imperative that the German infantry break through at Parpach and secure the Soviets' deep anti-tank ditch so that 22nd Panzer could cross. At this point 30th Corps would swing north to cut off those Soviet forces massed in the northern salient. In the meantime the 42nd Corps and Romanian 7th Corps had to convince the enemy that the main attack was coming in the north so that he would not have time to react to the trap developing in the south. Manstein was well aware that it was easy for the Red Army to reinforce Kerch and that this bridgehead constituted the main threat to 11th Army. To support the attack at Parpach, a battalion was despatched from Feodosiya in assault boats to land behind the enemy positions at daybreak.

On 8 May 30th Corps got across the anti-tank defences and penetrated the enemy's forward positions. Likewise the seaborne attack took the Soviets by surprise. However, the ground beyond the anti-tank obstacle proved impassable for

22nd Panzer. The tanks were not ready until the following day and then had to fight off a Red Army armoured counter-attack. On the opening day of *Trappenjagd* the Luftwaffe flew over 2,000 sorties.

The weather then closed in and the rain denied the German ground forces close air support. Nonetheless, they pushed east, keeping the Soviets off balance, and on 11 May the panzers reached the northern coast, trapping eight Soviet divisions against the Sea of Azov as they went. Six days later Kerch fell.

Manstein recalled:

> All the roads were littered with enemy vehicles, tanks and guns, and one kept passing long processions of prisoners. The view from a hill near Kerch, where I had rendezvoused with General von Richthofen, was quite breath-taking. Down below us, bathed in glorious sunshine, lay the Straits of Kerch – the goal we had dreamt of for so long. From the beach in front of us, which was crammed with Soviet vehicles of every possible description, enemy motor torpedo-boats made repeated attempts to pick up Soviet personnel, but they were driven off every time by our own gunfire.

Pockets of Soviet troops continued to resist along the coast, but artillery ensured that the battle for the Kerch Peninsula was over by 18 May, although a few brave Soviets continue to hold out in local caves for several weeks. The Red Army lost 170,000 prisoners, 3,800 vehicles, 1,133 guns, 300 aircraft and 258 tanks. So comprehensive was the defeat that few Soviets managed to reach the safety of the Taman Peninsula in the Kuban. Luckily for Manstein he had achieved his goals, because 8th Air Corps was now redeployed north to help deal with Soviet attacks in the Kharkov area.

(Opposite, above) German non-commissioned officers warm themselves during the Crimean night.

(Opposite, below) A crude but effective Soviet propaganda poster. In the winter of 1941 Stalin proposed a two-pronged attack against Manstein's occupation of the Crimea. This involved landings in the east at Kerch and to the southwest at the port of Feodosiya.

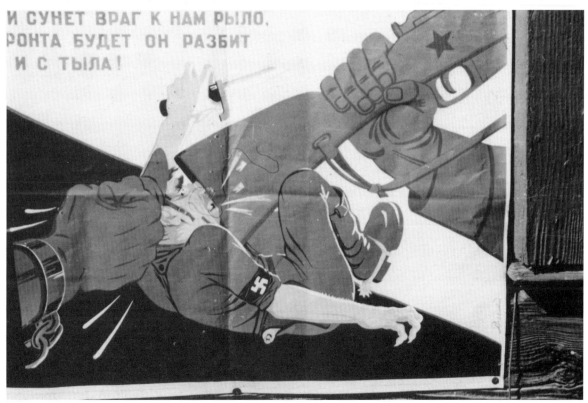

A German machine-gun team prepare to go on patrol. Although the Crimea enjoys a Mediterranean-type climate, snow does fall during the winter, especially in the mountains.

A German field kitchen does the rounds – mud rather than snow tended to restrict movement in the Crimea.

This German soldier looks to be wearing an improvised winter overcoat. The German 46th Infantry Division was the only Axis unit defending the Kerch Peninsula at the time of the Red Army's attack.

The Soviet cruiser *Molotov* with the Black Sea Fleet supported the Kerch-Feodosiya landings. On 9 November 1941 she fired almost 200 180mm shells at Axis positions near Feodosiya.

On 29 December 1941 the Soviet cruiser *Krasnyi Kavkaz* landed troops at Feodosiya harbour and was hit seventeen times by Axis artillery and mortar fire. She then ferried reinforcements to the Kerch bridgehead on 1 and 3 January 1942. Although damaged by German dive-bombers, the cruiser managed to limp back to Novorossiyk for repairs.

Molotov firing in anger. From 24-28 December 1941 the cruiser helped ship the 386th Rifle Division from Poti to Sevastopol. On 29 December she suffered damage from German artillery fire and retaliated with 205 180mm and 107 100mm shells. *Molotov* continued to support Soviet units on the Kerch Peninsula until 20 March 1942 when she returned to Poti for repairs.

Soviet fatalities caught by Axis shelling and air attack. In mid-January 1942 Manstein launched his counter-attack against the Soviet's Feodosiya beachhead. Within a matter of days it had been overrun with the Red Army's eight divisions being cut to pieces, losing 6,700 dead.

This Soviet T-26 light tank has thrown its farside track and one of its dead crew is visible in the foreground. The Red Army lost eighty-five tanks at Feodosiya.

The elderly battleship *Parizhskaya Kommuna* (formerly the *Sevastopol* – pictured after the war) supported the Kerch-Feodosiya landings, bombarding German positions during January, February and March 1942. Having worn her guns out she returned to Poti and took no further part in the war. This First World War-vintage battleship had originally been based at Sevastopol, but was evacuated to Novorossiyk in late October 1941 after the Germans breached the Perekop defences.

Soviet prisoners dressed in the basic 1939 khaki cotton shirt or *rubaha*, with stand-and-fall collar and breast patch pockets with buttoned flap. Although 10,000 Soviet soldiers were captured at Feodosiya the Red Army was able to strengthen its foothold at Kerch by crossing the ice from the Taman Peninsula. By February 1942 there were at least nine Soviet divisions and two tanks brigades poised on the Parpach line northeast of Feodosiya.

A knocked-out Soviet armoured car. Through February and March 1942 Soviet forces in the Kerch peninsula exhausted themselves trying to break through German defences at Parpach.

These two Soviet soldiers were killed in the open. On 8 May 1942 Manstein launched Operation *Trappenjagd* (Bustard Hunt) to drive the Soviet 44th, 47th and 51st Armies from Kerch. The 51st Army was successfully trapped at Ak-Monai north of Parpach.

A Panzer Mk IV belonging to the 22nd Panzer Division photographed in the Crimea in May 1942. Initially this newly-raised armoured division did not perform very well.

Manstein's destruction of the Soviet Crimea Front in the space of ten days resulted in the capture of 170,000 enemy troops, such as these men.

More grim looking Soviet prisoners. So comprehensive was the Red Army's defeat at Kerch that few survivors reached the neighbouring Taman Peninsula.

Two Soviet rifles mark the fallen. The Luftwaffe played a key role in Operation *Trappenjagd*, strafing and bombing the Soviet infantry units.

Soviet prisoners are made to help bury the German dead. The man on the left nearest the camera is wearing the older M1936 helmet which was derived from the French Adrian design.

The former defensive positions of two Red Army soldiers are thoroughly searched for useful intelligence or souvenirs.

To add to Stalin's woes, on 13 May 1942 the *Fidonisy* class destroyer *Dzerzhinsky*, serving with the Black Sea Fleet, struck a mine and sank.

Dzerzhinsky's sister-ship *Shaumyan* had been lost the month before.

Chapter Four

Hero City

Once again, thanks to the Crimean mountains, Manstein had little choice but assault Sevastopol from the north and on the southern part of the eastern defences. These operations were to be conducted by 54th Corps and 30th Corps respectively. In the middle the Romanian Mountain Corps was to act to pin down the enemy. The Romanian 18th Division was tasked with local attacks. In the north the first challenge was to secure the northern shore of Severnaya Bay and the heights around Gaytany. To the south they needed to capture the heights at Zapun either side of the roads from Balaclava and Sevastopol.

Supporting the northern attack were 121 artillery batteries that included a 420mm siege gun, two gigantic self-propelled 600mm mortars and a massive 800mm railway gun. The latter, known as 'Dora', had been designed to tackle the fortifications of the French Maginot Line but was not ready in time. To get it to the Crimea required laying a special railway and sixty trains. Manstein observed, 'Undoubtedly the effectiveness of the cannon bore no real relation to all the effort and expense that had gone into making it. Nevertheless, one of its shells did destroy a big enemy ammunition dump buried 90 feet in the natural rock on the northern shore of Severnaya Bay.' The southern assault was backed by fifty artillery batteries and Panzer Regiment 300 equipped with explosive remote-controlled tanks for breaching minefields and destroying fortifications.

By the evening of 1 June 1942 the Luftwaffe's 8th Air Corps had returned and was deployed unhindered by the Red Air Force at airfields north of Sevastopol. It brought with it four fighter groups, three dive-bomber groups, seven bomber groups, a long-range reconnaissance squadron and two tactical reconnaissance squadrons – a total of some 600 aircraft. This gave Manstein complete air superiority: Soviet forces in Sevastopol could muster only about sixty aircraft. Understandably, Manstein could not have been happier, noting, '8th Air Corps was the most powerful and hard-hitting Luftwaffe formation available for support of military operations. Its Commanding General, von Richthofen, was certainly the most outstanding Luftwaffe leader we had in World War 2.' This complacency almost cost him his life. Just before the attack on Sevastopol whilst intelligence-gathering,

Manstein was nearly killed. Aboard a torpedo-boat from the Italian 101st Squadron he went to scout the coastal road to see if it could be shelled by the Soviet fleet. On the way back two Soviet fighters strafed his vessel. Seven of the sixteen people on board were killed or wounded. Amongst the fatally wounded was Manstein's driver, Fritz Nagel, who had been with him since 1938.

Manstein's opening aerial and artillery bombardment of the Soviet defences began on 2 June 1942 and did not stop for five days and nights. General von Richthofen's pilots conducted up to 1,000 sorties a day, putting hundreds of aircraft into the air. On 2 June the Luftwaffe committed 723 aircraft, the following day 643, on 4 June 585, on 5 June 555 and on 6 June 563. In five days the 8th Air Corps dropped 2,264 tons of explosives and 23,800 incendiary bombs in the Sevastopol area. Soviet positions were bombed, artillery and anti-aircraft guns being particularly singled out. The city's water and electricity supplies were cut off, adding to the garrison's discomfort caused by a shortage of food.

Early on 7 June the defenders were subjected to another punishing bombardment by the Luftwaffe's dive-bombers and Axis artillery. Thanks to this, on the first day of the assault the Germans crossed the Kamyshly gully and the Belbek Valley. The Soviets were slowly forced from their strongpoints and in some cases fought to the very last. The main blow came from the northeast across the Mackenzie Hills, with a simultaneous attack via Zapun-Gora against the south-eastern outskirts of the city.

With their backs to the sea, the defenders fought doggedly. General T. K Kolomiyets' 25th 'Chapayev' Division from Odessa holding Defence Sector III, Colonel A. G. Kapitokhin's 95th Division and Colonel I. A. Laskin's 172nd Division both in Defence Sector IV and Colonel P. F. Gorpishchenko's 8th Marine Brigade and Colonel Y. I. Zhidilov's 7th Marine Brigade all fought with distinction. Women also helped to defend the city including the sniper Lyudmila Pavlichenko, the machine-gunner Nina Onilova and the scout Maria Baida.

Colonel von Choltitz's 16th Infantry Regiment, part of the 22nd Infantry Division, took Fort Stalin on 13 June. Four days later the strongpoints of the second defence line were in German hands. By this point 30th Corps had driven a wedge into the Zapun positions, but the Germans were at the limits of their endurance and to make matters worse the High Command wanted to redeploy the 8th Air Corps to Ukraine if Sevastopol did not fall quickly. Launching their final phase in the north, 'Maxim Gorky I' was captured and to the south the Germans gained a foothold in front of the Zapun Line. By 26 June 11th Army had captured nearly all of Sevastopol's outer defences.

Three days later German assault boats crossed Severnaya Bay to unhinge the Zapun defences. The German 50th Infantry Division had already captured Inkerman east of Sevastopol on 28 June and with the capture of the Heights of Inkerman and the penetration of the Zapun defences the fate of the fortress port was sealed. The German 28th Light Division broke through, taking the English Cemetery to the southeast. The 72nd Infantry Division pushed up the south coast, rolling up the Zapun with the capture of Windmill Hill, whilst the 170th Division struck west for the Khersones Peninsula. Swinging behind Balaclava, the Romanian 4th Mountain Division took 10,000 bedraggled Soviet prisoners.

By late June Sevastopol's surviving aircraft were redeployed to airfields in the Northern Caucasus and the anti-aircraft gunners fired their last remaining shells. Sevastopol lay wide open to air attack. It was bombarded on 1 July but the bulk of the defenders had already withdrawn west behind the defences of the Khersones Peninsula. There was no massed naval evacuation for the Soviet troops.

Captain Herbert Pabst, commanding Stuka Group 77's training group, flew up to seven dive-bomber missions a day against Sevastopol. He recalled:

> The mountain was terribly ploughed up by the heaviest bombs, craters metres deep, torn armour plating and shattered concrete walls. The dead were lying there, black and mangled in the blazing sun . . . Farther to the east could be heard the shrieking of dive-bombers attacking the firing positions at Inkerman. . . . Amid the fire the Soviets remained in the rocks, and continued to fire, but their fire was nothing compared to the tremendous impact of thousands of tons of bombs hailing down upon their rocky retreats without let up.

'Maxim Gorky II', defended by several thousand men, was captured but resistance on the Khersones lasted until 4 July when 30,000 men surrendered. In total Sevastopol yielded 90,000 prisoners. Manstein was now master of the Crimea and was promoted by Hitler to field marshal.

Despite this crushing defeat the Soviet authorities celebrated the heroic defence of Sevastopol; thirty-seven of the bravest defenders were awarded the title of Hero of the Soviet Union, and the medal 'For the Defence of Sevastopol' was awarded to 39,000 people. Sevastopol itself was made a Hero City. There was no denying the defenders had pinned down the German 11th Army, upsetting Hitler's plans for Operation *Blau*.

Manstein's victory meant Hitler was in control of the shortest route into the Caucasus via the Straits of Kerch. Turkey became amenable to waiving her neutrality more frequently by allowing of Axis ships carrying ammunition and other war-related materials free passage through the Bosporus.

After the capture of Sevastopol Manstein was not happy that 11th Army was redeployed from the southern wing of the Eastern Front to the far north and

Leningrad. His view was that an opportunity was lost and that 11th Army should have crossed the Kerch Straits into the Kuban to trap those Red Army forces falling back from the lower Don in the Caucasus in the face of Army Group A. Either that or it be placed in reserve with Army Group South – if this had happened 11th Army could have come to the help of 6th Army trapped at Stalingrad and the dramatic turning-point on the Eastern Front potentially avoided.

A 420mm German siege mortar bombarding Sevastopol. These weapons were capable of shattering concrete and delivered death and destruction.

German officers spotting for artillery during the bombardment of Sevastopol in June 1942. For the northern attack on the city, the Germans deployed 121 batteries, including the largest gun in history, the 800mm railway gun 'Dora'.

A Soviet casualty lays dead, grasping either a letter from a loved one or a map. Manstein's opening aerial and artillery bombardment on Sevastopol started on 2 June 1942 and lasted for five days and nights.

Dug-in Soviet infantry coming under attack. The wheeled 7.62mm Maxim M1910/30 on the Vladimirov mount was the Red Army's standard heavy machine gun and was used throughout the war.

German infantry moving forward, having just captured three Soviet prisoners. Severnaya Bay and the Zapun line were vital to the defence of Sevastopol and had to be breached by the Germans.

Silhouetted against the sun, German troops look down on this Red Army soldier killed in the Kamyshy gully.

Soviet casualties seeking assistance. By 28 June 1942 Manstein's forces had captured the Inkerman Heights and pierced the Zapun defences, leaving Sevastopol open for the final assault.

The Germans decided to reduce their casualties by first pounding Sevastopol with artillery and bombers before entering the city. This reduced great swathes of the city's buildings to derelict shells.

Surrendering Soviet officers. The second man from the left is having a final cigarette before going into captivity. The Romanians, swinging in behind Balaclava, captured 10,000 prisoners in one go.

Soviet troops examining the latest bomb damage. By the end of June Sevastopol's anti-aircraft gunners had run out of ammunition and could no longer fend off the Luftwaffe.

In early July 1942 the battered Soviet garrison abandoned bombed-out Sevastopol and withdrew to the promontories west of Streletskaya Bay and to the Khersones Peninsula to the southwest for one final stand.

Cowed-looking Soviet prisoners. The man on the far right appears to have been badly burned.

Once the German 30th Corps had taken Windmill Hill and the 'Maxim Gorky II' battery at Cape Fiolent, the Axis forces were closing in on the Khersones Peninsula.

Soviet dead collected for burial.

Local civilians being checked to make sure they are not hiding Red Army stragglers. They include at least five males of fighting age who would have aroused suspicion.

The wrecked turret of one of the 'Maxim Gorky' batteries.

The destruction wrought on Sevastopol harbour.

On 4 July 1942 the remnants of the Soviet Separate Coastal Army surrendered on the Khersones Peninsula. Around 30,000 men laid down their arms.

The defeat of the Soviet garrison at Sevastopol resulted in some 95,000 casualties, with around 20,000 killed.

This peasant family faced an uncertain future under the German occupation, which was to last two years.

German riflemen fire a salute over their fallen comrades. Total Axis casualties from November 1941 to mid-July 1942 were over 71,000.

Manstein's reward for capturing Sevastopol was promotion to Field Marshal.

Like the rest of the towns and cities in the western Soviet Union, those in the Crimea were left in ruins after the campaigns of 1941-42.

The cruiser *Komintern*. After delivering supplies to the 44th Army at Feodosiya in January 1942, she transported reinforcements to Sevastopol. She was damaged by air attack on 11 March and again on 2 July at Novorossiysk and was finally sunk at Poti fourteen days later.

During mid-June 1942 the Soviet cruiser *Molotov* successfully ferried reinforcements into Sevastopol and wounded out. On 2 August she was caught off Feodosiya by Heinkel 111 torpedo bombers and Italian torpedo boats which blew her stern off, but she managed to limp back to Poti.

Chapter Five

Kerch-Eltigen Operation

The third component of Hitler's summer offensive of 1942 was codenamed Operation *Blau III* (Blue 3). This was undertaken by Field Marshal Wilhelm List's Army Group A formed from the southern elements of Army Group South. On 7 July 1942 1st Panzer Army and 17th Army were launched forward between Izyum on the River Donets and Taganrog on the Sea of Azov to provide right-flank protection for 6th Army's drive through the 'Donets Corridor' towards Stalingrad to the northeast Their objective was to capture the area as far south as the River Don between Tsimlyansky and Rostov.

Army Group A was so successful that its offensive was extended to a drive into the Caucasus with the aim of securing the vital oilfields at Maikop and Grozny, the Black Sea port of Batumi near the Turkish frontier and the Caspian port of Baku. It was halted along the line of the Terek River by 18 November by strong resistance from the Soviet Caucasus and Transcaucasus Fronts.

Now that the Crimea was secure, 11th Army should have crossed the Straits of Kerch in support of the 17th Army's efforts to take Maikop and Batumi. Instead Hitler now decided that 11th Army should not be deployed to the Kuban as planned but to the very other end of the Eastern Front where it could help with the capture of Leningrad. Clearly he felt if a port city needed to be stormed then 11th Army was the one for the job. In reality the army was largely broken up with one corps left to garrison the Crimea whilst 30th and 54th Corps moved north with all the heavy artillery and four infantry divisions. The 11th Army's other supporting units were redeployed as reinforcements to places as diverse as Smolensk and Crete. What was planned as a five-division attack from the Crimean Peninsula to the Kuban took place on 2 September 1942 on a much smaller scale. In fact, the Germans attack only managed to penetrate south along the coast as far as Novorossiysk.

At the end of 1943 the Red Army fought to liberate the Ukraine west of the Dnieper. The 1st, 2nd, 3rd and 4th Ukrainian Fronts massed 2.3 million men, 2,040 tanks and self-propelled guns, 28,800 field guns and mortars and 2,370 aircraft, with which to smash Manstein's Army Group South and Kleist's Army Group A, which could muster some 1.7 million troops, with 2,200 panzers, 16,800 field guns and 1,460 aircraft. Soviet partisans numbering 50,000 men in the Ukraine, Crimea and Moldavia played their part pinning down ten divisions and thirty police battalions.

With the Red Army sweeping west General Erwin Jaenecke's 17th Army was cut off in the Crimea by the end of October 1943. Airlifts by Ju 52 transport aircraft and later He 111 bombers from 4th Air Fleet were used to supply Jaenecke's trapped troops. Surprisingly these flights were conducted with very few losses from Soviet action. Just five Ju 52s were lost between 5 November 1943 and 2 February 1944.

Undeterred by its defeat at Feodosiya and Kerch the Red Army decided to conduct further ad hoc amphibious operations in the Crimea. This was facilitated by the withdrawal of German and Romanian forces from the Taman Peninsula to the east of the Kerch Straits. Such an operation would gain a lodgement ready to liberate Sevastopol. The plan was to carry out a major landing in the north at Yenikale near Kerch with a southern diversionary assault carried out near the town of Eltigen.

The Soviet 4th Ukrainian Front oversaw the attack, deploying the 18th and 56th Armies supported by the Black Sea Fleet and the Azov Flotilla. General Ivan Petrov, commanding 56th Army, was in overall charge, with Vice Admiral Lev Vladimirsky responsible for naval operations. Jaenecke's forces consisted of the 5th Corps in the north and the 49th Mountain Corps holding the Perekop Isthmus, with the Romanian Mountain Corps defending the southern Crimea.

Initially poor weather and rough seas hampered Soviet schedules. Then on 1 November 1943 Colonel V. F. Gladkov's 318th Rifle Division from 18th Army and the 386th Naval Infantry Battalion came ashore at Eltigen. Romanian forces in the area were driven off and a bridgehead established. Two days later the 2nd and 55th Guards Rifle Divisions as well as the 32nd Rifle Division from 56th Army under covering artillery fire from the Taman landed at Yenikale. They were followed by the 383rd Rifle Division on 7 November and by 11 November the Yenikale beachhead held 27,700 Soviet troops. The German 5th Corps and the Romanian 3rd Mountain Division were unable to crush this foothold in the Crimea.

In contrast, the diversionary attack did not go so well. The 117th Guards Rifle Regiment was landed at Eltigen to reinforce the 318th Division, but they managed to get only just over a mile inland. German naval forces in the shape of the 3rd Minesweeper Flotilla proceeded to cut Eltigen off from the sea. A number of Soviet nighttime supply runs were made but these were intercepted and those supplies that were landed were insufficient to sustain the beachhead. When the Red Air Force attempted to help by dropping supplies they were pounced on by Luftwaffe fighters.

Axis forces squeezed Eltigen for five weeks before overwhelming the Soviet beachhead on 6 December 1943. This attack conducted by Romanian troops supported by German assault guns struck from the west, while cavalry of the 6th Division conducted diversionary attacks from the south. The Soviet defences collapsed the following day, with the 318th Division having lost 1,200 dead and 1,570 captured along with thirty-eight tanks and twenty-five anti-tank guns.

Around 820 Soviet troops escaped from Eltigen and headed north for Yenikale. Overrunning some German artillery positions they occupied Mount Mithridates. This enemy force behind his Yenikale frontlines understandably alarmed Jaenecke and the Romanian 3rd Mountain Division was tasked with eliminating it. A number of Soviet soldiers did reach the coast and were evacuated by the Azov Flotilla to Opasnoe, a village in the Yenikale beachhead. By 11 December the Romanians had defeated the remaining Soviet troops on Mount Mithridates.

In the meantime Soviet naval forces continued to strengthen the Red Army units at Yenikale. By early December the bridgehead contained 75,000 men supported by 128 tanks, 582 guns, 187 mortars and 764 trucks. Just as important, they had managed to get almost 10,000 tons of ammunition ashore. These forces pushed inland to within reach of Kerch. This left the Axis forces in the Crimea facing the prospect of fighting a two-front battle to the north at Perekop and to the east at Kerch.

A Romanian pilot with his IAR-80 fighter. In the summer of 1943 the IAR-80s returned home to provide air defence over Romania's oil fields and to fly convoy escort duties over the Black Sea.

An Italian-built Savoia-Marchetti SM.79-JR belonging to the Romanian air force. Once the Red Air Force had regained control of the skies over the Kuban the Axis lost its dominance over the Crimea and the Black Sea.

After the redeployment of the German 11th Army to Leningrad, General Erwin Jaenecke's 17th Army withdrew into the region from the Taman peninsula. By the end of 1943 his forces had been cut off.

Fortunately for the Axis forces trapped in the Crimea in early October 1943, Stuka dive-bombers caught the destroyers *Besposhchadny*, *Kharkov* (shown) and *Sposobny* after they had been shelling Yalta and Feodosiya. All three were sunk following four attacks. As a result Stalin forbade the Black Sea Fleet to deploy large naval vessels without his express permission.

Wrapped up against the cold, a German soldier keeps watch for the enemy. After liberating the Caucasus and southern Ukraine in early November 1943 the Red Army sought to end the Nazi occupation of the Crimea with landings at Eltigen and Yenikale on the Kerch Peninsula.

This German soldier is guarding a 37mm anti-tank gun.

Soviet troops from the 2nd Guards 'Taman' Division armed with PPSh 41 submachine guns landing at Yenikale seven miles east of the town of Kerch on 3 November 1941. Two days earlier Soviet forces also landed at Eltigen.

Eltigen was recaptured on 7 December 1943 after the Soviet 318th Rifle Division was overwhelmed.

While German forces moved to contain the Yenikale beachhead, Romanian forces attacked the Eltigen beachhead, calling in artillery and air strikes.

German troops bury their dead.

A German foot patrol keeping busy on occupation duties. During the winter of 1943-44 Axis forces could only watch as the Red Army built up its strength at Yenikale and north of the Perekop isthmus.

German equipment on the move.

Conditions in the Crimea Mountains were often harsh. Keeping the isolated outposts resupplied was no easy task, especially with the ever-present danger of partisan attacks.

German troops question Soviet prisoners. One man has been singled out for interrogation which was likely to include a beating if he did not cooperate.

Interrogation time for three Soviet prisoners. The recapture of Eltigen meant yet more Soviet prisoners falling into Axis hands. The Soviet 318th Division suffered 1,200 killed and captured as well as losing thirty-eight tanks and twenty-five anti-tank guns.

Men of the Kriegsmarine (German Navy) bury their dead. The Germans created their own Black Sea fleet by transporting twenty-three minesweepers, ten motor torpedo boats and six submarines down the Danube during 1942-43.

More German sailors – the German 3rd Minesweeper Flotilla was able to cut off the Soviets' Eltigen beachhead.

The German Navy was outgunned in the Black Sea but along with the Luftwaffe ensured that the Soviet Black Sea Fleet went into terminal decline by 1944 thanks to steady losses.

A German PoW goes off to an uncertain fate. By early December 1943 the Yenikale bridgehead contained 75,000 Soviet troops poised for the liberation of the Crimea.

A sad row of simple German graves left in the sandy soil.

Chapter Six

Perekop and Kerch Offensives

With the Red Army thrusting into western Ukraine General Erwin Janecke's 17th Army, cut off in the Crimea by the 4th Ukrainian Front and North Caucasian Front, faced destruction. The fate of his command was almost a repeat of 6th Army's at Stalingrad. Despite the strength of their formidable defences the prospect for the German and supporting Romanian forces, totalling around 195,000 men, equipped with 215 assault guns and self-propelled guns, 3,600 guns and mortars and 148 aircraft, was little short of grim.

After clearing the Black Sea coast to the mouth of the Dniester River, the Red Army was now well placed to liberate the Crimea. Common sense would have dictated it was a good time to evacuate Jaenecke's command before the inevitable blow fell. Instead, Hitler was adamant that holding the Crimea was necessary to safeguard Romanian oil and to keep Turkey neutral.

General Jaenecke was in an unenviable position. Hitler wanted Sevastopol held as a fortress but the city's inner defences had been left in ruins since the 1941-42 campaign. Jaenecke had been at Stalingrad and understood perfectly well what happened when a surrounded and unsupported army was ordered to hold its ground to the last. He had not been idle, however, and his troops had done all they could to reinforce their outer defences. He had confidence in the fortifications behind which his eleven divisions held Perekop, Kerch, the Ak-Monai positions and Sevastopol itself. The lagoons of the Sivash Sea had not frozen and they seemed to present the Red Army with a considerable obstacle. The Romanians left only a covering force to screen the salt flats and marshes and dug in on the nearby high ground.

The German 49th Mountain Corps, commanded by General Rudolf Konrad, defended the northern Crimea, with the German 50th Infantry Division blocking the Perekop Isthmus and German 336th Infantry Division and the Romanian 10th and 19th Infantry Divisions south of the Sivash Sea. In reserve supporting these units were the German 111th Infantry Division and Mountain Regiment Krym. The

German 5th Corps, commanded by General Karl Allmendinger, was deployed at Kerch to the east, consisting of the German 73rd and 98th Infantry Divisions and the Romanian 3rd Mountain and 6th Cavalry Divisions. The Romanian 1st Mountain Corps was on coastal defence and anti-partisan duties.

The Red Army planned a two-pronged assault in the spring of 1944. Tolbukin's 4th Ukrainian Front, attacking from the north, and Yeremenko's Separate Coastal Army striking from the eastern end of the Kerch Peninsula, could field 470,000 men, 559 tanks and self-propelled guns, and almost 6,000 field guns and mortars. General K. A. Vershinin's 4th Air Army assigned to Yeremenko and General T. T. Khryukin's 8th Air Army assigned to Tolbukin with a total of some 2,255 aircraft backed up the ground assault. The Germans claimed 604 Soviet aircraft over the Crimea in the six months leading up to their evacuation, with one Luftwaffe pilot remarkably claiming 247 of the kills!

Tolbulkin planned to strike across the Perekop and the Sivash lagoons, employing G. F. Zakharov's 2nd Guards Army and Kreizer's 51st Army respectively. His intention was that the main attack would come through the lagoons, bringing his forces into the rear of the German units in the Perekop, followed by a drive on Simferopol and Sevastopol. The Sivash operations required engineers and pontoons in order to traverse water so salty horses would not enter it. At the other end of the Crimea General Yeremenko's Coastal Army would drive into the interior from its bridgehead and liberate Kerch, destroying the Axis defences and blocking the escape route through Ak-Monai, pinning down the Germans to stop them interfering with Tolbukin's attack.

The push into northern Crimea started on 8 April 1944 just as Odessa was being liberated. The 4th Ukrainian Front launched the assault across the Perekop Isthmus followed by the Kerch attack the following day. At 0800 Soviet artillery in support of the 2nd Guards opened fire on the German 50th Infantry Division's positions. Two hours later the 51st Army's guns opened up on the German 336th Infantry Division and the Romanian 10th Infantry Division in the Sivash sector.

Under cover of a smokescreen, Zakharov's guardsmen forced their way into Armyansk while Kreizer's infantry ferried their artillery and light tanks on pontoons across the salt lagoons. Once across the Sivash the goal was to come ashore at the southern end of the ruined Chongar Bridge. After the rafted artillery and vehicles were clear of the water they were to strike out into the rear of the Axis Perekop defences. The right flank of the German 49th Mountain Corps quickly crumbled once the 10th Romanian Infantry Division collapsed.

Intensive night bombing attacks over Kerch were a prelude to the 4th Air Army's mass strikes in support of the Separate Coastal Army's invasion. A special forward command post was set up from where the Deputy Air Army Commander, General

Slyusarev, directed fighter cover over the beachhead. The Soviet Coastal Army reached Kerch on 11 April. The following day it secured the Ak-Monai position which constituted the last fortified German line of defence on the Kerch Peninsula. On the 13th the Coastal Army liberated the city of Feodosiya, followed by Sudak to the southwest two days later.

On 12 April Axis forces had hastily withdrawn to Sevastopol, seeking the protection of its fortifications. As they went the Soviet 19th Tank Corps and other mobile units continually attacked them. Mountain Regiment Krym, part of the 49th Mountain Corps, made a stand at Dzhankoy to cover the escape south. The Soviet 4th and 8th Air Armies constantly pounded the Crimean ports and hit ships at sea. In the Black Sea Soviet submarines and torpedo boats attacked enemy convoys. Partisans also caused upheaval with attacks behind the Axis lines. By 16 April the German 17th Army was in full retreat toward Sevastopol.

In the air the Luftwaffe struggled to contain the Red Air Force. In the Perekop area between 12 and 18 April 4th Air Fleet managed 530 sorties. These peaked on 14 April with 150 but for the rest of the week it could only offer 40-60 sorties a day. Then, having exhausted themselves, the Luftwaffe was unable to offer any further serious resistance to enemy aircraft or advancing troops.

Once 17th Army was squeezed into the southwestern corner of the Crimea there was little the Luftwaffe could do to help. On 13 April, Simferopol, the Crimean capital, was liberated by Kreizer's 51st Army with 19th Tank Corps taking the honours. This meant that German and Romanian aircraft were confined to the few airstrips in the Sevastopol area. The Red Air Force bombed and strafed German defences in Sevastopol continually. These attacks were supported by Soviet artillery, which came into range after 17 April. For six days the Soviet 8th Air Army pounded the defences of Sevastopol, dropping over 2,000 tons of bombs and 24,000 anti-tank munitions. By 20 April the Soviets had air superiority: the main Sevastopol airfield could no longer be used by the Luftwaffe and some 200 aircraft, most of which were fighters, had to be written off once the last main airstrip was overrun on 8 May.

In eight days Soviet pilots conducted well over 13,000 sorties, some 2,000 were against the Axis air and sea evacuation that had commenced in mid-April. The Red Army reached the outskirts of Sevastopol toward the end of the month. Jaenecke flew to Berchtesgaden to meet Hitler to persuade him not to sacrifice the remaining 65,000 men of 17th Army and authorise rescuing the Sevastopol garrison. Hitler was unmoved and General Allmendinger, commander of 5th Corps, replaced Jaenecke, but the Romanian-led evacuation continued.

The Germans desperately needed to keep the Soviet guns out of range of Sevastopol's docks and wharfs as equipment and men were now being shipped out in ever-growing numbers. This meant that the northern defences were vital and most of the mobile German artillery was deployed here. A smaller force of two divisions was deployed to the east and southeast to hold the formidable Zapun Heights.

In late April Zakharov's 2nd Guards began to attack from the north across the Mackenzie Heights, but Tolbukin then shifted his main attack to his left flank against the Zapun, with the 19th Tanks Corps sweeping from the south into the German rear. Its task completed, the headquarters of the 4th Air Army was transferred to the Second Belorussian Front and Vershinin's air regiments, now absorbed into the 8th Air Army, remained to take part in the storming and capture of Sevastopol.

The Guards opened the attack from the north on the morning of 5 May. They fought their way up the Mackenzie Heights and through an extensive German minefield. Two days later Tolbukin unleashed his main attack from the east. Kreizer's 51st Army crossed the Bakchisarai Mountains during the night and deployed before the northern slopes of the Zapun. The Soviet 77th Rifle Division under Colonel Rodionov was poised to strike once Colonel Pavlov's 12th Assault Engineer Brigade had cleared a route. The Coastal Army to the south had seized Balaklava and was also poised to assault the southern end of the Zapun. The 11th Guards Rifle Corps was to act as the spearhead for the final push in the southern sector.

By mid-morning Kreizer had gained a foothold on the ridge and the Red Banner was hoisted by a sapper from the 12th Assault Brigade. During the afternoon the 51st and Coastal Armies battled their way up the slopes and forced their way into the Inkerman valley. By this point the way to Sevastopol was open. In the northern sector German soldiers, after offering fierce resistance, were soon falling back towards Inkerman Bridge or the ferries. The 51st Army's spearhead, formed by the 10th Rifle Corps, was soon involved in heavy street fighting. From the Zapun Soviet troops fought their way into Sevastopol's outskirts, reaching the main station. By the evening of 9 May Sevastopol had been liberated.

Soviet T-34 tanks and supporting infantry in the Ukraine. The liberation of eastern Ukraine meant that by 1944 the Red Army was ready to retake the Crimea.

A handsome young Red Army company commander identifiable by the single stripe and two stars on his shoulder boards. In early 1943 Red Army uniforms were redesigned and this included the reintroduction of shoulder boards, the stand collar and rank markings, all of which were throwbacks to Tsarist uniforms. The chest patch pockets were removed and officers had slash breast pockets with a flap.

A confident-looking veteran Soviet senior sergeant in a studio shot probably taken for his family. He is also wearing the new-style uniform along with the *furashka* or peaked cap. By the winter of 1943 Stalin's rejuvenated Red Army had firmly turned the tide against Hitler's Wehrmacht.

A German MG34 machine-gun team await an attack. While the Axis forces had reinforced the Crimea's outer defences, Sevastopol's inner fortifications largely remained in ruins after the 1941-42 campaign.

A smiling German soldier posing in flooded Soviet trenches. In 1944 General Jaenecke's 17th Army had two German and two Romanian infantry divisions holding the old Soviet defences on the Perekop isthmus and the Sivash Sea.

A Soviet mortar crew contribute to the opening bombardment. Soviet forces massed 6,000 guns and mortars for the attack on the Crimea which began on 8 April 1944.

Heavy Soviet field guns such as these 152mm howitzers were used to pound the Axis defences in the Crimea.

The formidable 203mm howitzer was designed to deal with fortifications and was nicknamed 'Stalin's sledgehammer' by German troops.

Soviet rocket launchers were also used to deluge Axis positions with high explosives.

Soviet T-34 tanks and supporting infantry clearing enemy defences. The German 17th Army lacked panzers and had to rely on the assault guns and self-propelled guns supporting the infantry divisions.

Soviet infantry attacking under a covering bombardment. This was laid down on the positions of the German 50th and 336th Infantry Divisions and the Romanian 10th Infantry Division.

A German MG34 team open fire on a Red Army attack. The assault on the Perekop opened with the Soviet 2nd Guards Army striking the German 50th Infantry's positions.

A German infantryman emerges from his hiding place amongst the reeds. The Soviet 51st Army successfully attacked the German and Romanian units holding the Sivash lagoons and marshes.

The rear entrance to a well-concealed bunker. Once the Soviets had taken Armyansk the Perekop defences were breached.

German troops taking a look at knocked-out Soviet T-26 light tanks.

Another disabled T-26. The Soviet 19th Tank Corps liberated the Crimean capital of Simferopol on 13 April 1944.

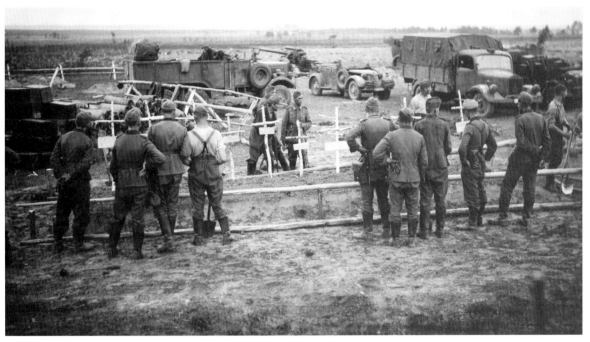

A German artillery unit bury their dead before withdrawing.

A destroyed German assault gun in Sevastopol is surrounded by Soviet troops. The city was liberated by the evening of 9 May 1944.

The shattered remains of a T-34 tank. Jaenecke claimed 17th Army knocked out 602 Soviet tanks between 8 and 23 April 1944.

Chapter Seven

Crimean Dunkirk

Hitler forbade a seaborne evacuation because he thought the Soviets would use the Crimea to launch air attacks against Romania's vital oil refineries. He also argued, not unreasonably, that 17th Army would be a thorn in the Soviets' flank. His delusion was that the Red Army would be thrown back and the Wehrmacht would link up with the 17th Army again, but instead he consigned it to a cruel and chaotic fate.

During mid-April to mid-May almost 121,000 men managed to escape the developing trap (half of whom were Germans). This was thanks to the bravery of the Romanian Royal Navy as well as the German and Italian navies operating out of Constanta some 220 nautical miles away. The Red Army liberated Odessa on 10 April 1944, cutting the shortest seaborne escape route for 17th Army. The success of this 'Crimean Dunkirk' came at a heavy cost, however. The Romanians dubbed the mission Operation '60,000' as this was roughly the number of Romanian troops still in the Crimea.

Two unsuccessful bombing missions against Constanta by the Red Air Force convinced the Soviets to concentrate their efforts against the evacuation fleet. Soviet submarines and warships supported by aircraft were directed to intercept those trying to flee across the Black Sea. There was little that the Luftwaffe units based in Romania could do to help. A few Fw 190 fighters from the Balkans, twin-engined fighters from Austria and torpedo bombers from the western Mediterranean were hastily redeployed - at most they could muster eighty aircraft. After the night bombing of Constanta a squadron of German night fighters was also sent to help.

Whilst Luftwaffe protection was weak after the loss of the airfield at Khersones it was non-existent over the Crimea giving the Soviets a free hand (the last transport planes flew wounded out on the morning of 9 May). Faced with a dangerous 24-hour round trip the Romanian Navy proceeded to play a highly-dangerous game of 'cat and mouse' with their pursuers.

The first convoy led by the Romanian destroyers NMS *Regina Maria* and NMS *Marasesti* arrived off Sevastopol on 12 April and despite air and submarine attacks returned to Constanta two days later with 4,361 men, including 3,197 Germans. In the first stage of the evacuation conducted between 12 April and 5 May two German submarine hunters, a tanker and a lighter were damaged. One Romanian destroyer, two armed transport pontoons and several transport ships were also damaged.

As the Red Army closed in, a last desperate bid was made to rescue those Axis forces squeezed into the Khersones Peninsula. It was only on 8 May as the Red Army was sweeping into Sevastopol that Hitler belatedly authorised the evacuation. Admiral Otto Schultz was the German naval commander overseeing operations at Khersones. A convoy including the cargo vessels *Teja* and *Totila* arrived off Khersones on 10 May and began to take on board German and Romanian soldiers. They weathered the first air attack but during the second raid the *Totila* was struck by three bombs and sank near Sevastopol with 5,000 evacuees aboard.

Tragically the *Teja* and her escorting Romanian destroyers could not stop to pick up survivors and sped on their way. The Red Air Force then proceeded to sink the *Teja* and of the 4,000 men who went into the water just 400 were rescued. Despite this disaster the evacuation from Khersones and Sevastopol continued. More ships arrived off Khersones in the early hours of 11 May. After sunrise Soviet bombers appeared and destroyed the ships *Romania* and Danubius that were carrying munitions. The German transport ship *Helga* ran aground and was also destroyed.

At Khersones the Romanian destroyer NMS *Regele Ferdinand* weathered thirty-three air attacks, which were repelled using her anti-aircraft guns and her 120mm main armament. A Soviet battery of 152mm guns began to target the ship, so her captain put her in reverse and returned fire with her main guns. On the return journey to Constanta the *Regele Ferdinand* rescued six Germans and two Romanians who had survived the sinking of the *Teja*.

The Soviet attacks were unrelenting. During the second stage of the evacuation between 6-13 May the Germans lost five ships, three tugs and two lighters and another vessel was damaged. Four German submarine hunters were sunk, as were three motorboats. Another six submarine hunters were damaged. Three large Romanian transport ships were sunk and two warships were damaged. Also, two Hungarian transport ships were damaged. Losses to the Luftwaffe during the airlift were surprisingly light, consisting of six He 111 bombers between 12 April and 11 May.

Despite the naval cost of Operation '60,000' in total 120,853 people were evacuated including 7,115 civilians, 2,581 prisoners and 15,391 Russian volunteers. These final battles cost the Axis forces some 57,000 men, a large number of who drowned. In particular the sinking of the *Totila* and *Teja* resulted in around 9,000 deaths.

A Soviet G-5 class motor torpedo boat. At the start of the war the Black Sea Fleet had almost 100 of these vessels. They tended to be used for escort and transport roles, making relatively few torpedo attacks. However, they sank a German submarine chaser and a Romanian minelayer.

Soviet motor torpedo boats on patrol in the Black Sea. As Stalin had forbidden the deployment of the fleet's larger vessels, it fell to the smaller boats and the Red Air Force to cut off the Axis sea routes.

Exhausted German soldiers pause for a cigarette. Once the German 17th Army had been driven from Sevastopol rearguard operations had to cover the retreat into the Khersones peninsula.

Retreating German infantry – their hope was that they would be rescued from Khersones either by sea or air.

A German truck negotiates the mud after a sudden downpour.

A German MG34 team prepare for a final stand. Having lost all their heavy equipment 17th Army had nothing with which to fend off Soviet tanks.

Exhausted German troops take a break from the fighting. Hopes that they could be evacuated from the Khersones airfield were soon dashed. Soviet air attacks and artillery closed the airfield and made it hazardous for ships to come in close.

The Romanian destroyer NMS *Regina Maria*. The Romanian Navy came to the rescue of the Axis forces trapped in the Crimea, collecting men first from Sevastopol and then Khersones. The *Regina Maria* led the first convoy to Sevastopol on 12 April 1944 and then to Khersones a month later.

The Romanian destroyer *Regele Ferdinand* braved thirty-three air attacks rescuing trapped Axis troops from Khersones.

The desperate battle for the Khersones raged for three days after the liberation of Sevastopol. Several divisional commanders were killed including one caught in Soviet tank fire.

A young boy caught up in the fighting receives first aid for a nasty wound in his thigh.

This German soldier faced an uncertain fate.

The evacuation to the Romanian port of Constanta included 2,581 prisoners and 15,391 Russian volunteers. Why they were taken instead of German or Romanian soldiers is unclear.

Chapter Eight

Death in Khersones

After the fall of Sevastopol the remaining Axis forces withdrew into the Khersones Peninsula for a last stand while as many men were evacuated by sea as possible. Stalin instructed Tolbukin on 10 May 1944 that the Crimea should be completely liberated within the next 24 hours. The Soviet Separate Coastal Army was tasked with clearing resistance on the Khersones. The aim was to affect a junction with the Soviet 19th Tank Corps. Soviet fighter-bombers, dive-bombers and artillery pounded those enemy troops escaping from Sevastopol by boat. They also targeted the last remaining airstrip still controlled by the Germans in the Khersones.

The remnants of the 17th Army tried beating off the Soviet Coastal Army using their remaining anti-aircraft guns firing over open sights. The situation was chaotic as Soviet artillery ranged freely over the remaining spit of land still held by the Axis. General Erich Gruner, commanding the German 111th Infantry Division and Paul Betz, acting commander of the 50th Infantry Division, were killed and the 336th Infantry Division's commander General Wolf Hagemann was wounded. Gruner was caught by Soviet tank fire.

The Black Sea was also a killing ground. Soviet aircraft strafed German and Romanian troops trying to reach the open water in small boats and on rafts in the hope of being rescued. At the same time warships and motor-gunboats of the Soviet Black Sea Fleet patrolled the Crimean coastline sinking any rescue ships that were foolish enough to come too close.

During the Axis' fighting retreat to Sevastopol, the Germans lost 12,221 men and the Romanians 17,652 along with most of their armour. Whilst the 17th Army held out in Sevastopol until 9 May, the desperate Axis resistance in the Khersones did not cease for another three days when the last 3,000 defenders were overwhelmed, Soviet artillery having prevented their evacuation by sea. Some 25,000 German troops surrendered at noon on the 12th. Many of them were gathered on the Khersones auxiliary airfield at the northern end of the peninsula, which under German occupation had been used as a Luftwaffe repair facility.

To the very last the Romanian Navy strove valiantly to rescue as many as it could.

At 2100 hours on 12 May a final convoy arrived off Khersones – four more were organised but never despatched once word of the surrender became known. This force was led by the Romanian destroyer NMS *Regina Maria* and the minelayers NMS *Dacia* and NMS *Amiral Murgescu*. They soon came under sustained artillery fire but the *Dacia* proceeded to take on board soldiers from four armed transport pontoons. Soviet aircraft using flares proceeded to bomb the ship killing and wounding a number of the crew. At 0130 hours, with 1,200 people aboard, the engines failed for a nerve-wracking 20 minutes. Once underway at daybreak on 13 May *Dacia* was attacked by Soviet torpedo bombers, but she scattered then using her 105mm guns. At 1600 hours the battered ship finally steamed into Constanta.

NMS *Regina Maria*'s captain sailed close to shore to rescue 650 men from a transport pontoon and then caught up with the *Dacia*. On 13 May the last Romanian ship to depart Khersones was the NMS *Amiral Murgescu*. This vessel rescued 1,000 soldiers and General Walter Hartmann, the last commanding officer of the bridgehead. Admiral Schultz escaped aboard a motor torpedo boat. Major General Hermann Böhme, commander of the 73rd Infantry Division, was not so lucky and was captured that day along with most of his division. Lieutenant Colonel Alexander Franz, in charge of the remains of the 111th Infantry Division, was also taken prisoner with many of his men.

While about half of the 17th Army escaped across the Black Sea, approximately 117,000 were killed, wounded or captured. The Germans lost 65,100 causalities (31,700 dead and missing in action and 33,400 wounded). Their Romanian allies lost 31,600 (25,800 dead and missing and 5,800 wounded); some 20,000 local Soviet 'volunteers' suffered an unknown fate. Soviet casualties during the offensive amounted to some 83,000 men, 171 tanks, 521 artillery pieces and 179 aircraft. The 4th Ukrainian Front suffered the highest losses with 13,000 killed and 50,000 wounded and the Coastal Army 4,000 killed and 16,000 wounded.

Hitler's insistence that his isolated troops defend a precarious position instead of evacuating as soon as humanly possible created a futile drain on already overstretched Luftwaffe resources. During 599 air engagements during the Battle for the Crimea the Luftwaffe lost 297 aircraft, with another 200 destroyed on the ground.

The Soviet authorities claim during their offensive west of the Dneiper in Ukraine and in the Crimea, the Red Army destroyed ten divisions and forced the Germans to dissolve another eight, while a total of sixty-eight German divisions lost 50 to 60 per cent of their manpower. It seemed impossible to conceive that the Wehrmacht could weather such bloodletting. In the aftermath Army Group A was re-designated Army Group South Ukraine and Army Group South became Army Group North Ukraine.

At the end of April 1944 Stalin's deputy commander Georgiy Zhukov noted:

Even though throughout the winter and spring campaign, the actions of our forces had resulted in signal victories I felt the German troops were still strong enough to put up a stiff defence on the Soviet-German front. As far as the strategic proficiency of their High Command and the local army group commands were concerned, after the disaster in the Stalingrad area and particularly after the Kursk battle it had drastically declined.

Unlike the first phase of the war, the Nazi Command had become sluggish and lacked ingenuity, particularly in critical situations. Their decisions betrayed the fact that they were unable to correctly assess the capacities of either their own troops or those of the enemy. The Nazi Command would often be too late in withdrawing its forces from under the threat of flanking blows or encirclement – and this, of course, placed these in a hopeless situation.

His comments on the Red Army's victory in the Crimea were perfunctory. 'An offensive by the 4th Ukrainian Front, the Independent Maritime Army and the Black Sea Fleet culminated in the complete rout of the Crimea group of enemy forces. On 9 May the Hero City of Sevastopol was freed, and on 12 May the operation to liberate the Crimea was completed.'

'Hitler's decision to hold the Crimea was one of his most insane inspirations,' wrote American war correspondent Alexander Werth. He saw the liberation of the Crimea as a clear indication that German morale was faltering and concluded:

It will remain one of the great puzzles of the war why, in 1941-42, despite overwhelming German and Romanian superiority in tanks and aircraft, and a substantial superiority in men, Sevastopol succeeded in holding out for 250 days and why in 1944, the Russians captured it within four days ... Was there not something lacking in German morale by April 1944?

The hapless General Jaenecke was held responsible for the loss of the Crimea and the unauthorised evacuation. Upon his arrival in Romania he was arrested and court-martialled. General Heinz Guderian was instructed to investigate the case and Jaenecke was acquitted in June 1944. The following year the Soviets arrested him and he served ten years' hard labour before being released in 1955. He had tried to spare his men the horrors of the Perekop, Sivash and Kerch, but to no avail, and the Soviets held him and Manstein responsible for the terrible destruction in the Crimea.

The shattered remains of the great port of Sevastopol. The Red Army liberated it on 9 May 1944.

Stalin ordered that the larger warships such as this destroyer be kept out of harm's way but they were soon patrolling the coastal waters of the Crimea as the Axis forces fled toward Constanta.

German troops trying to save the last of their precious supplies. What was not evacuated was destroyed.

As in the next photograph, this German position consists of little more than a hole dug in the soft sand.

A grim-looking machine-gun team struggle to keep the Red Army at bay. Note their lack of personal equipment, indicating perhaps that they were poised to abandon their position as soon as possible.

Apprehensive German officers await evacuation. General Hartmann was the last commanding officer of the Khersonnes bridgehead, whilst Admiral Schultz oversaw the maritime evacuation. Both escaped.

Men of the Kriegsmarine captured at Kerch under the watchful eye of a Soviet sailor. Their expressions are a mixture of defiance and fear. The German army was very critical of the navy's evacuation efforts and was highly displeased that Admiral Otto Schultz was awarded the Knight's Cross for his role as naval commander in the Crimea.

This German sailor and soldier were caught trying to get out into the Black Sea on a makeshift raft in the desperate hope of being picked up by the Kriegsmarine or the Romanian Navy.

The face of defeat – the sailor is made to pose for the camera.

German prisoners mingle with local civilians displaced by the fighting.

A poor-quality Soviet photo showing Axis dead at Khersones.

Captured anti-tank and flak guns at Khersones.

Abandoned assault guns and self-propelled guns at Khersones.

Soviet casualties gathered at a first-aid station. In liberating the Crimea the 4th Ukrainian Front suffered 50,000 wounded and the Separate Coastal Army another 16,000 wounded.

German prisoners waiting to go into captivity. Some 25,000 German troops surrendered at Khersones on 12 May 1944 marking the end of the battle for the Crimea.

Understandably the Black Sea Fleet was keen to play its role in the liberation of Sevastopol. It would not be until early November 1944 that the battleship *Parizhskaya Kommuna* led the remaining major surface vessels back to the port.